	DATE DUE		
OCT 0 4 1999			
NY 07 '03			
DE 11 '03			
OC 26 '04			
OC 25 '05			
OCT 0 7 08			
JAN 2 3 '09			

SUPERSTARS OF FILM

pamela anderson lee

Esme Hawes

CHELSEA HOUSE PUBLISHERS
Philadelphia

First published in traditional hardback edition
© 1998 by Chelsea House Publishers.
Printed in Hong Kong
Copyright © Parragon Book Service Ltd 1995
Unit 13–17, Avonbridge Trading Estate, Atlantic Road
Avonmouth, Bristol, England BS11 9QD

Illustrations courtesy of Aquarius; Hulton Deutsch Collection;
Retna Pictures Ltd.

Library of Congress Cataloging-in-Publication Data
Hawes, Esme.
    Pamela Anderson Lee / by Esme Hawes.
        p.   cm. — (Superstars of film)
    Originally published: London : Parragon Books, 1996.
    Filmography: p.
    Includes index.
    Summary: A biography of the 'Baywatch' star whose
television and movie career and tumultuous lifestyle have
made her the focus of public attention.
    ISBN 0-7910-4647-8 (hc)
    1. Lee, Pamela Anderson, 1967-   —Juvenile literature.
    2. Actors—United States--Biography—Juvenile literature.
    [1. Actors and actresses.] I. Title. II. Series.
PN2287.L33H38   1997
791.45'028'092—dc21
    [B]   97-24535
                                                        CIP
                                                        AC

CONTENTS

Pamela in Baywatch

EARLY YEARS

Pamela Anderson Lee—the undisputed star attraction of *Baywatch*, one of the world's most popular television programs—was born July 1, 1967, in a one-moose town called Comox in the Canadian province of British Columbia. A small harbor settlement with less than 6,000 inhabitants, situated 90 miles northwest of Vancouver, Comox may boast the wild grandeur of Vancouver Island as a backdrop, but it is a quiet town. When Pamela was growing up there, it couldn't claim to have much more than the local 7-Eleven as a nighttime hotspot for bored teenagers.

Barry Anderson, Pamela's father, had arrived in Comox some ten years earlier looking for work as a chimney sweep. In fact he found employment in such diverse occupations as a sawmill worker and manager of a boiler maintenance company. His wife, Carol, spent her time working as a long-suffering waitress in Wrangler's Diner, a hamburger joint. She expended most of her energy coping with her poorly paid job, and her marriage was at best uneasy. Barry was a quiet, moody individual who drank excessively for most of their marriage and Pamela had always filled an emotional void in her life.

Though her home territory was unremarkable, Pamela's arrival in the world was immediately auspicious. She was born on Centennial Day—one of Canada's most important national anniversaries. The local newspaper went hunting for babies born on this special day and Pamela, just a few hours old, made her front-page debut. Carol Anderson was ecstatic. This was the most exciting event that had ever happened to anyone in her family and she was thrilled to promote her newborn baby as cover girl material. Carol was later quoted in interviews admitting that she encouraged Pam to get out and be noticed from the very start: "It was my prayer that she wouldn't be a timid soul like me, living in a small town and working as a waitress. I pushed Pam and her brother Jerry [who is four years younger] to do the things I'd been afraid to do, and it worked. They became little hams and adored all the attention."

After this encouraging start, however, Pamela went through her childhood and early teens in traditional fashion, developing into a typically awkward adolescent—a gawky tomboy with fly-away mousy hair who was forced to suffer the temporary indignity of braces to straighten her teeth. There was no hint of the glamorous, sexy woman Pamela was to become. There was also no sign of the sassy confidence that defines Pamela Anderson the international star, so adored by millions of fans today. When family friends came to visit and Carol pressed Pamela and Jerry into performing the party pieces they'd rehearsed under her direction, Pamela would blush, stammer, and sometimes hide behind the sofa. None of this seems to have moderated Carol Anderson's understandable ambitions for her children and she insisted that both take lead roles in the school play. She has recalled that they both enjoyed themselves so much that they refused to leave the stage after they'd delivered their lines. "They were such scene-stealers that the teacher had to come on stage and drag them off." She has also characterized her daughter's behavior during this period as "stubborn."

Pamela's contemporaries have different recollections of that time. "She was a quiet little thing," her school friend

Sandra James has been quoted as saying. "But she had this dream that one day she'd break away." In interviews now, all that Pamela seems able to recall of these early years was that her family lived in an unremarkable six-bedroom house on Douglas Street and were forced to follow a lifestyle dictated by low income. Pamela has commented, "People who say that money doesn't matter obviously already have it. My parents have struggled their whole lives. I recently paid off the three mortgages on their house and bought them a new car."

In most respects Pamela's teenage years passed normally. She attended Highland Secondary, the local high school, where she was an average student, having the usual small group of girlfriends with whom she would share secrets. But no one else particularly noticed her. On the day she graduated from high school in 1985, Pamela, following in her school's grand tradition, filled out a questionnaire about her future that was to be published, along with everyone else's, in the school's yearbook. The very first question on the form was, "Describe your desired destiny," to which she replied with the single word "Stewardess." She then had to answer the demanding question "What do you think you'll really end up doing when you grow up?" "California beach bum," she replied, after which she listed her main hobbies as "suntanning and weightlifting." Her school gym coach, Pat Lewis, noticed this remark in the yearbook and commented that, although Pamela was, by this stage, rather cute-looking and highly competitive, he remembered no special skills or talent that made her stand out from the rest of her class. Again, she seems to have been a pretty normal girl, even if the interest in weightlifting suggests she had already begun working on her physical image.

In the next blank space, Pamela had to nominate her "weakness." She later told friends that she had absolutely no hesitation about the answer to this question. Her weakness, she said, much to the giggling admiration of her high school chums, was "dark-tanned guys in Levi 501s (especially Ty)." Tyron Anderson, the class heartthrob, was astonished by this piece of news. In his entry he had already listed his main interest in life as "girls in skimpy bikinis," but he was totally taken aback by Pamela's public declaration of interest. Until that moment, he had been completely unaware of their apparent harmony and Pamela had been far too shy ever to have expressed an interest in the class stud.

Now employed as a tire-fitter in Vancouver, Ty still keeps a collection of love letters that Pamela wrote to him after they started going out together. He has allowed a number of these to appear in tabloid newspapers, along with a variety of photos from the "early years"—before Pamela became a blonde and submitted to plastic surgery. "The natural Pamela was a lot more attractive than the image that's been created for her," he says, "and I want to remember her like she is in these photos."

But back in the summer of '85, it was all love and roses. The pair became the high school love match, and after they graduated Ty got his first job, as a fireman in Red Deer, Alberta. Pamela, who was deeply smitten with her first real boyfriend, immediately followed the dictates of her heart and also went to Red Deer, where she acquired a job at the local gym as a weight trainer. The young couple lived there peacefully enough for a year, and then Ty decided that it was time to move on, to tackle life head on. He applied for a job in Canada's most happening city—Vancouver, British Columbia—and, once again, Pamela dutifully followed him and set about finding a new job for herself. She began work as a receptionist at a travel agency and, in the evenings, she had a part-time job as a fitness instructor. The pair had now been coexisting comfortably for almost four years and life seemed to be going quite well for them.

And then fate intervened. One sunny Saturday afternoon in spring 1988, Pamela, who had nothing much else to do, decided on the spur of the moment to head over to the local soccer match, a home game for the British Columbia Lions of Vancouver. That morning she just happened to have pulled on a T-shirt with a Labatt's beer logo emblazoned across the chest. It was a casual fashion decision that was to change her life forever. Pamela was an enthusiastic soccer fan, and as soon as the slightly dull match started, she began to jump up and down enthusiastically and to shake her very evident assets for all they were worth.

During one of the many quiet moments on the field, a TV cameraman decided to liven up the action by focusing on anything interesting he could find in the audience and, quite randomly, his lens happened to settle on blonde and bouncing Pamela. Suddenly, a huge close-up of Pamela Anderson was projected onto the massive scoreboard video screen on the wall of the stadium. The crowd went mad, and the rest is history. By coincidence, an advertising executive from Labatt's was present at the match, and witnessed the moment of absolute hysteria over the girl in his firm's T-shirt. He immediately spotted a top business opportunity and the hunt for the girl was on. Within a few weeks he had managed to track down the anonymous beauty and he offered her a contract and a permanent part on the beer team. At last Pamela had the chance to fulfill her dream of never having to return to Comox. From that day forward she was to become known across the entire nation as the "Labatt's Blue Zone Girl." She proved a hugely successful and eye-catching marketing image for the company as posters began appearing on billboards all over Canada. Back in Comox, Carol Anderson—convinced that all her early ambitions for Pamela were being realized overnight—described the Labatt's campaign as "like a dream come true. It was fantastic."

Pamela, too, was delighted. Her life was utterly transformed and, for the first time in her life, though she wasn't yet rich, she wasn't struggling either, and on several occasions people even recognized her on the street. It was an exciting time for the girl from the countryside. The poster of Pamela firmly grasping the neck of her bottle of beer was now planted in the imaginations of people all over the country, a number of whom spotted its obvious potential. One of these happened to be a *Playboy* photographer, who tracked down her telephone number and gave her a call. It would make him very happy, and her a good bit wealthier, he said, if she would agree to sign up for a day's shooting of nude photographs for *Playboy* magazine.

Pamela wasn't so sure. She called her parents to discuss the matter and told her father that she wasn't happy about taking all her clothes off but she realized the experience could buy her a ticket to the wider world. Pamela's parents thought that her assessment of the situation was correct, and very soon *Playboy* had written a check to the Anderson family. Just a few days later, Pamela and her mother found themselves on a plane, jetting their way straight to Los Angeles, where the shoot was to take place.

Playboy paid for Pamela and Carol to stay in a luxury hotel and both were excited and impressed. Though Pamela had initially balked at the prospect of taking off her clothes and had turned down the offer of a centerfold spread, she was still paid around $6,000 for the photo session. Any initial misgivings her mother may have had were dispelled by the experience itself. The *Playboy* staff, said Carol, "were wonderful people. They even gave Pam her own bodyguard. I certainly didn't have any qualms about it. They can't get enough of her."

Carol was right. In fact, by 1995 Pamela had become the first woman in the history of *Playboy* to have been photographed for the magazine five times—more often than Sharon Stone and enough to win her tremendous approval in Hollywood. That first time on the set, however, Pamela was very nervous about the whole experience. She was wearing an English striped blazer with nothing underneath and was terrified of the moment when she had to take it off.

Superstars of Film

As the shoot went on, however, she began to relax and relish all the attention. She even started playing up to the camera. The *Playboy* team was delighted and so was Pamela. "When I saw the photographs," she said, "I was stunned. I'd always thought of myself as geeky and unattractive. Suddenly, with the right lights and the setting, I looked like a goddess."

Pamela knew straight away that her heart now lay in Los Angeles and that she wanted to stay in the city of dreams forever. So as soon as she could, she withdrew the money she had been paid by *Playboy* from the only bank in Comox and moved permanently to the sunny state of California. Left in Vancouver, Ty was devastated. "I guess everyone has a soft spot for their first love," he said, "it's just that mine turned out to be Pamela Anderson." Many years later, when he was watching television one evening, Ty saw his first girlfriend being interviewed on a talk show and held his breath as she was asked the key question, "And who was the first love of your life?" Pamela replied that it had been Scott Baio, the actor who had initially made his name in the hit TV series *Happy Days*. She did not mention her old high school beau. But Ty apparently took it in stride, saying, "Well, I guess that's the name of the game in the big city."

On the beach with Pamela and the cast of Baywatch

ROAD TO FAME

Meanwhile, back in the big city, the very first thing that Pamela did with her *Playboy* nest egg was to invest most of it on cosmetic surgery. "When I came to Los Angeles," she said, "everybody I met had implants. I got caught up in it . . . . I thought . . . it would give me a fuller figure. But I was so disappointed—it wasn't worth all the pain and I'm still the same bra size." She soon endured further plastic surgery in order to acquire much fuller lips. She also began dyeing her hair a paler shade of blonde.

By the end of 1989 Pamela had not only accepted the offer of her first *Playboy* cover but had appeared in her first centerfold. By this time her objections to nudity had virtually disappeared and she soon found herself to be a very popular girl. She hired an agent, who began to receive calls from all sorts of people inviting her out on dates. At Christmas time she received her first invitation to one of the legendary parties thrown by *Playboy* owner Hugh Heffner at his mansion. Only the very rich, the very famous, or the very beautiful were asked to those parties and Pamela now qualified in the last of these categories. In time, of course, she would make it to Heffner's "A" list on all three counts. For now she was still new to the fame game, self-protective and unsure of her ground. But she relished her new role and went to everything to which she was invited.

One evening, during one of the groovy Heffner parties, a rather good-looking young man stepped up to her shyly and waved a copy of one of her *Playboy* centerfolds in her face. "I've found you at last," murmured her lovesick fan. Pamela learned that he had been trying to track her down for weeks and that he was an actor named Scott Baio, who'd once played a character named Chachi in the TV series *Happy Days*. Pamela had watched the show as a child and was really thrilled that such an important person might be interested in her. They talked all night and Scott soon told her that she was the most beautiful woman in the world. Pamela was touched and excited and agreed to go on a date with the good-looking star. It soon turned out, however, that Scott just wasn't romantic enough for Pam. "The chemistry was never there," she said later, and she was bitterly disappointed when, on their first Valentine's Day together, he gave her a matching pair of floor mats for her car.

Scott absolutely adored his new girlfriend and begged her to move into his Hollywood home. She finally agreed to do so during 1990 and always describes her ex-boyfriend as "a great guy—just not the great guy for me." She also admitted, "In the end I realized I wasn't in love with him," and, by the end of 1991, though he asked her repeatedly and publicly, she knew that marriage to Scott would be a disaster and moved out of the house. Pamela says she always knew that she had made the right decision and his juvenile response to her moving out merely confirmed this for her. And, while his star continued to fade, hers just grew and grew. Only a few months after the breakup with Scott, she was offered her first big acting break—a small but significant role in the TV sitcom *Home Improvement*. Playing the character of Lisa the Tool Girl, each week she had a star moment when she handed over the "tool of the week" to the star of the country's highest-rated new sitcom. Pamela had really begun to be noticed.

By January 1992 Pamela also had regular work in TV

Superstars of Film

advertisements and modeling assignments. At one of these, a jeans commercial, she encountered an actor named David Charvet, who was to become the next big love of her life. "He was very young," she said, "and wet behind the ears. I taught him how to love." David was much more romantic than Scott. He wooed Pamela with candlelit dinners and flowers and gave her the red-carpet treatment.

The pair was still together when Pamela was spotted on *Home Improvement* by David Hasselhof, the coproducer and star of the popular television series *Baywatch*. Erika Eleniak, who'd been the first female star of the show, had become fed up with the flimsiness of both the role and her costumes and had now left to appear in the film *Under Siege* with Steven Seagal. The new *Baywatch* series was about to start shooting and the production team was in a panic, desperately seeking a replacement actress to fill in for the departed star. They were looking for someone to play a new lifeguard character named CJ Parker and had already auditioned thousands of girls. Every starlet in Hollywood seemed to want the role and almost all of them had already turned up for a screen test. Pamela, however, was on a roll. Her popularity was riding high and she had just appeared on her third *Playboy* cover. David Hasselhof was an acute appraiser of female assets and, within a few weeks, Pamela had been offered the part of a lifetime. She jumped at the opportunity. The role, she said, was far more challenging than that of Lisa the Tool Girl in *Home Improvement*.

But she also knew her own value and demanded that she be contracted to appear in every episode of the show. Pamela realized that this was her chance at the really big time. When she signed on for *Baywatch,* she knew she had been transformed from a small-town girl who'd played a few bit parts into an international star. The moment her pen left the paper she ran to the telephone and called Canada. "Mum," she said, "I think that you and the rest of the folks at home are gonna be proud of me some day." They already were.

Pamela with Baywatch *costar David Charvet*

FAME AND FORTUNE

A few months later David Charvet also joined the cast of *Baywatch*, though the couple was now spending more time apart. In May 1993 Pamela began work on a straight-to-video thriller called *Snapdragon*, starring herself and an actor named Steven Bauer, who had once been married to Melanie Griffith. Sitting at home alone, knowing that Pamela was spending hours rehearsing love scenes with her costar Steven, David Charvet felt confused and neglected. "I was trying to focus on my first movie," grumbled Pam, "and I'd come home and, instead of being supportive, David would argue. The pressure just built and built and the last time I saw him was when he was moving his things out of my house. David's a very sweet guy, but this movie really worked against us as a couple." Pamela, now famous, was once again alone.

Footloose and fancy-free, she quickly embraced her single-woman status and embarked upon a string of high-profile love affairs, reiterating to any number of newspapers the phrase that she had uttered so memorably in answer to her school yearbook questionnaire all those years ago. "I have always loved men," she said, "it's a bit of a weakness for me. I just can't leave them alone."

"Dating in L.A. is very difficult," she cried repeatedly, and then launched into the activity with gusto, recovering from the split with David Charvet by crying on the muscular shoulders of a number of hunks, including *Rambo* man Sylvester Stallone. "I met Sly through friends," she said at the time, "but it's just a social thing. He's a dinner-friend really." Dinner with Sylvester was soon over and Pamela, feeling a little bruised, agreed to meet her old boyfriend, Scott Baio, for a brief, reconciliatory dinner. Scott turned up to the restaurant looking hopeful. But this time, instead of flashing his old copy of *Playboy* at "the most beautiful woman in the world," he rapidly whipped out a diamond ring. "I just wasn't thinking straight," she says, "I wasn't even dating Scott. He just took me out for dinner. An hour after I had said yes to his marriage proposal I knew I had to undo it all."

Pamela returned the ring and went back to filming episodes of *Baywatch,* which continued to see increased audience ratings by the week. Given its growing appeal, she was becoming ever more famous and more and more men began to call her for dates. One of these was Dean Cain, star of the TV series *Lois and Clark.* "Ooh! Those eyes, that face, that body," she gushed to her friend, Sandra Reeves. The tabloids were soon publicizing the relationship. Pam was besotted with Dean and pursued him all over town, lavishing expensive gifts on him and tracking his every move. Dean, however, turned out not to be the long-term boyfriend type and the more Pamela tagged along, the more irritated he became. He finally called a halt to their relationship and began dating someone else. Friends say that Pamela abandoned all pride as she desperately tried to win Dean back, even though it was obvious that the Princeton University graduate had lost interest in her. She filled his answering machine with impassioned messages, none of which he bothered to return, until one day he called to demand that she stop bothering him. "You are simply not my intellectual equal," he said. "Please stop calling me." Pamela was devastated and, typically, elected to go public with her grief and

On the beach with Baywatch *actor David Charvet*

anger. Dean Cain, she told the tabloids, was now one of the ex-lovers she preferred not to think about. "We all make mistakes," she said. "We're not friends right now."

Subsequent romances included one with MTV host Eric Nies, but when he was caught cavorting with her fellow *Baywatch* star Nicole Eggert, he swiftly became another ex-boyfriend Pamela no longer thought about. Pamela's love life was beginning to look bleak and she even talked about giving up men altogether. Hope resurfaced, however, during a new round of *Baywatch* filming, when Pamela met world-champion surfer Kelly Slater. He had a guest role in a few episodes as an aspiring surfer, and Pamela, in her lifeguard role, helped to save his life when he became tangled in some underwater barbed wire. Although the pair got along well, nothing happened until November 1994, when Pamela flew to Hawaii to film a special *Baywatch* TV movie called *Hidden Paradise*. Slater soon discovered that Pamela was in town and the pair linked up and renewed their acquaintance. They got along famously and Kelly soon managed to talk Pamela into hosting the Coca-Cola Surf Classic competition in Australia. During their fortnight's stay in the Antipodes the couple was inseparable. Once more Pamela had high hopes of true love.

She returned to Malibu, where she celebrated some of her newfound purchasing power by buying a two-bedroom beach house for about a million dollars. She now shared her home with her brother, Jerry, who had followed her to California, and with her cat, Petty, and her golden retriever, Star. Despite the fact that everyone in town knew that she was now dating Kelly, men were still constantly phoning her agent and asking Pamela out on dates. Pamela began to feel some of the negative effects of fame and now employed a round-the-clock team of security guards to ward off both the identified and the unidentified stalkers who constantly pursued her. Realistically, she told journalists, "I'm not going to complain about the price of fame.

Superstars of Film

I knew what I wanted when I set out to become a star and I knew that there would be drawbacks."

And she was right. She was now a huge star and *Baywatch* was officially watched by more than a billion viewers in over 142 countries. And most of these people tuned in each week merely to watch Pamela race across the California sands wearing her red lifeguard suit. However, since her main function in *Baywatch* was to look beautiful, she was also paying the price for this concentration on the physical. Her contract expressly forbade her from gaining or losing a single pound. If her body shape changed in any way she had to pay a substantial on-the-spot fine, and each episode of *Baywatch* now contractually bound her to show a minimum of 154 cleavage shots, which totaled up to three close-ups of Pamela's bosom every minute. "I don't mind if they make a big fuss of my figure," she says. "I love the dumb blonde image. I have nothing to live up to."

In the meantime, things were going relatively well with Kelly. Being a fitness freak himself, he encouraged Pamela in her health regime, and in order to maintain her figure the couple took to rising at 5:30 every morning. Pamela would start off her day's training with a half-hour session with her private karate instructor. The pair would then split up for their day's activities, and during her lunchbreak Pamela would get out her rollerblades and perfect her in-line skating skills. She would then smother her hair with conditioners and sunproof gels to maintain its finely tuned beach coloring. After finishing work, she would return home each evening and practice a ritual that involved taking a relaxing, hour-long bath surrounded by aromatherapy incense and candles. Pamela seemed at last to be on an even keel, and it showed. *Baywatch,* which had achieved only low audience ratings after its first season and was due to be axed after just one year, was now being syndicated to over 165 television stations in America alone. And Kelly Slater was charming company on the road to mega-fame.

"He's so polite," she told friends, "he calls everyone 'Sir' or 'Ma'am' and sends me flowers every day."

Kelly was very supportive and never let her down. "No gain without pain," he told her first thing every morning as they jogged to the beach, surrounded by security guards, frantically bounding through their planned aerobics schedule. Since his recent signing with the prestigious William Morris Agency, Kelly had just become surfing's first-ever superstar, had signed a million-dollar contract with a surfwear company, and was inundated with film offers. Their life together seemed like a dream, but Pamela was soon heartily sick of paradise.

Kelly was supplanted in Pamela's affections when she embarked on a brief liaison with the forty-eight-year-old producer of *Batman*, Jon Peters, a one-time hairdresser to the stars who'd risen to the very top of the Hollywood heap via a string of hit movies. "Jon has proposed to me dozens of times," she said. "He's got tons of money but I said, 'I want nothing from you. If I make it in this town, I want to make it on my own.' He respects that. We're still best friends, we always will be." And that was that.

Pamela with Baywatch *costars*

Pamela with heavy metal rocker Brett Michaels

MARRIAGE

In 1994 Pamela found a new beau in the form of an American rock star named Brett Michaels, who was the lead singer in the heavy metal band Poison. His most significant role in her life, however, was that he took her to a New Year's Eve party to welcome in 1995. This was the party at which she first met one of Brett's wild and crazy rock friends, a drummer named Tommy Lee. Tommy and Pamela were instant dynamite. They immediately greeted each other enthusiastically, and the drummer of the heavy metal band Motley Crue immediately knew that this was something special. "It really bugged Lee," said one of his cronies, "that she was seeing Brett. He kept boasting, 'One day he'll be history. One day she'll be mine. I'm going to marry that girl.'" Pamela soon dumped Brett, and on February 15, 1995, she took advantage of a break in *Baywatch* filming to zip off to Cancun, Mexico, to take part in a photo shoot for a pinup calendar.

Tommy Lee (a man with MAYHEM tattooed in eight-inch Gothic letters across his stomach), seized the moment, dropped his girlfriend (model Bobbie Brown), and took the next plane to Cancun. On his arrival at Pamela's luxury hotel, he plagued the flustered receptionist with requests to be put through to her suite. Pamela knew all about Tommy's "rock-pig" reputation and initially refused to take any of his

Pamela with her pal Star

calls. She knew that he had previously been married to Heather Locklear, the woman who played the scheming Sammy Jo in the television series *Dynasty*, and she knew that Heather (whom Pamela closely resembled) was Tommy's second wife. She also knew that Tommy had told reporters that he had proposed to Heather because she wore "the tightest, shortest rubber miniskirts I ever laid eyes on." The marriage had apparently ground to a halt in 1993 when Locklear finally tired of Tommy's mercurial mood swings, but Pamela was perfectly aware of Tommy's reputation for juvenile and often violent behavior.

The omens were not good. Pamela asked hotel security to eject him from the lobby and to turn him away if he ever tried to come back. Tommy just continued to call. Finally, after forty-eight hours of unceasing pressure, Pamela relented and agreed to speak to her number one fan. After some negotiation she reluctantly allowed Tommy Lee to take her away from the posh Camino Real Hotel in Cancun to the La Boom! nightclub, a well-known local hot spot.

"It was a real Boom!" she said. "From the moment we got there . . . it was instant, mind-blowing animal attraction. The sparks were literally flying—it was electric, dynamic, like a charge flying between us. When he proposed, I didn't stop to think." The pair drank champagne until eight the next morning and, just four days later, on Sunday, February 19, they realized Tommy's dream when they were married on the local beach. Pamela was clad simply in a classic white bikini; Tommy wore his swimming trunks. The witnesses included two of Tommy's pals from L.A., Bobby Fernandez and Doug White, and an anonymous woman who had been at La Boom! with the party the previous evening and had won the "Miss Bikini" competition. The ceremony was performed by a Mexican judge, Pedro Solis, who described Pamela's outfit as "a touch on the micro side." The couple filled out the registration form and handed in the proper documents, and then Judge Solis read them a poem by a

Tommy Lee

Mexican philosopher about the importance of their vows. One particularly emphasized extract went: "Marriage is the only legal way of founding a family, of preserving mankind, and of avoiding the imperfections of the human soul."

As soon as vows were exchanged, Tommy picked up his new bride and raced her down to the sea. Tommy was quoted as saying that it was "the coolest day, man. We hired jet-skis and raced around in the water and then we went back to the hotel . . . It was the best day of my life."

Remarkably, Pamela and Tommy's marriage seemed able to survive the readiness with which the tabloids publicized their fights, grievances, and most intimate moments. Comments that could easily be construed as libelous, and would be expected to do some damage to other relationships, failed to come between them. For them apparently, "no publicity is bad publicity." Pamela is quoted as saying, "I hope people get a good laugh out of that tabloid stuff, because they've got to know it's not true." This kind of negative coverage began only a few days into their honeymoon when Tommy, who is reputedly worth many millions, reportedly asked Pamela to sign a prenuptial agreement he'd had his lawyers prepare in draft form and fax to him at the Camino Real Hotel. Pamela, who was worth barely $2 million at this time, was devastated by this development and responded by telephoning her mother and complaining, "Tommy doesn't love me, Tommy doesn't trust me, Tommy thinks the marriage is bust." The prosaic explanation for Tommy's move was that he was already paying huge sums of alimony to Heather Locklear and simply didn't want to be caught short again. He wanted things sorted and he wanted them sorted now.

The newlyweds had a vigorous and very public fight in the middle of the hotel lobby. Other guests took sides and joined in. Pamela's mother, meanwhile, was said to be devastated by the match. She stated that she was "shocked speechless" by news of the wedding. "We didn't know she was even dating him," she said. "In fact, we didn't know who he was. Our first reaction was that they must have the wrong girl." It was too late to quibble now, however. Pamela was still her daughter, after all, and what she needed was motherly comfort. "This is the first decision I have ever made totally on my own," she told her parents and they weren't about to tell her it was a bad one. But this maternal sympathy didn't preclude Carol Anderson from holding a highly publicized press conference. "I just don't understand this," she said, "Pamela is essentially a milk and cookie girl. That's the way she's always been—very sporty, a very clean girl. She's always brought her boyfriends home to meet me—all except this thing she's married. I don't know him but everyone says he does drugs and things. Quite honestly he looks like a mother's nightmare with that ring in his nose." However, since then Carol Anderson has been quoted as saying, "We'd heard that he was wild, but we were pleasantly surprised. He turned out to be a perfect gentleman. And he certainly makes Pam happy."

Having discussed the nuptial agreement issue at length with her understanding parents, Pam's retaliatory move on Tommy was to locate the home telephone number of his former wife, Heather Locklear. Thinking it must be a crank call, Heather asked Pamela for descriptive details of Lee's more intimate tattoos, which Pam, of course, gave her with 100 percent accuracy. With the code cracked, Pamela went on to ask her what she thought about the agreement. Heather had heard through the grapevine that Pamela idolized her, and was therefore quite well disposed toward her caller. She had recently married rock guitarist Ritchie Sambora, and while there was now no love lost between Heather and Tommy, Heather advised Pamela to sign the document. Her advice came with a word or two of warning. "You've gotta watch out for yourself, girl," she said, and proceeded to give Pam some serious advice about her new relationship. On no account was she to let Lee visit her on any TV or film set, since he always had to be the center of attention, which could be very distracting when Pam was trying to work. Publicly Heather told journalists, "I wish Tommy a lot of luck . . . but I wish Pam even more. He cheated on me the entire time we were married and he's going to do the same thing to Pam. He hasn't changed a bit." Heather felt sorry for Pamela, and most of Heather's friends gave the marriage a maximum of six months.

Pamela and Tommy Lee

AFTER THE WEDDING

The couple flew back to L.A. a few days later. Within days they were preparing to move into a brand new $4 million dream mansion in Malibu that Tommy had bought just days before the wedding. Their new neighbors would be Steven Spielberg and Arnold Schwarzenegger, but Pamela was concerned only with Tommy. "Tommy and I went mad for days," she said, "I was in love for the first time."

But pressure was put on the new marriage almost immediately when Pam began work on her real movie debut, an action thriller called *Barb Wire,* which she prepared for by having a tattoo of some barbed wire etched into her upper arm. Unwisely, she ignored Heather Locklear's solid advice and invited Tommy to accompany her to work every day. It was only a matter of time before tabloid editors and Hollywood gossip columnists were gleefully receiving calls from others working on the film with tales to sell. Naturally these were quickly passed on to their scandal-hungry readers, who lapped up every juicy tidbit.

The lovebirds were, it seems, driving the *Barb Wire* team mad, publicly kissing and making doe eyes at each other. Worse—and just as Heather had predicted—Tommy's presence was disruptive, especially to Pamela. She was taking her job very seriously and was desperate to be recognized as a "real" actress. Those at the shoot were quick to fault the

Pamela displaying her barbed wire tattoo

influence of Tommy Lee on set, although director David Hogan countered this by saying, "Tommy never disrupted a day of shooting. If he did, I wasn't aware of it." Pamela, who was feeling overwhelmed by her first major film role said, "I'm glad Tommy was there. Tommy actually helped me out a lot."

Though *Barb Wire* was eventually finished, filming had been a fiasco. The negative publicity was intense and, at the end of the day, America's movie critics had little positive to say. In a way, they were missing the point. Pamela Anderson had long since ceased to be a mere actress. No matter how disparaging the reviews were, she knew that she was an international star. She had joined the elite who are famous for being famous. Proof of that came in abundance in May 1995 when she turned up at the forty-eighth Cannes Film Festival to promote *Barb Wire* and created a riot. When she walked along the promenade wearing a typically skimpy outfit, the crowds went wild. "She's done nothing, but she's already stolen the show," said one of the organizers. "We kid ourselves that the festival is about a serious debate on film. Then Pamela Anderson mania takes over. It's a joke."

It wasn't a joke for Pamela. She was thrilled to be taken seriously at last particularly since, back in Los Angeles, the bad news continued to come thick and fast. Her *Baywatch* stunt double was fired for telling an interviewer that her own breasts, unlike Pam's, were real. And, more ominously still, the nonstop party lifestyle she and Tommy enjoyed was beginning to take its toll on her health. Just a few weeks after her return home from Cannes, she was rushed to the hospital with acute abdominal pains. Initial tests revealed a burst ovarian cyst, while secondary tests confirmed that she was pregnant. Pamela was ecstatic, only to suffer the tragedy of a miscarriage just a few weeks later. The early months of her marriage to Tommy had not been a bed of roses.

But Pamela was a fighter, and just two days after she was released from hospital, obsessed with her role in *Barb Wire,* she was back on the set ready to reshoot a few final scenes. She went on record to say that she was determined to become pregnant again as soon as possible. "I just want to have a baby," she told reporters. Part of the reason for this wish was apparently that she now believed that fatherhood would be the only way to tame troublesome Tommy, now thirty-three and still determined to party.

Having finished work on *Barb Wire,* Pamela went back to filming *Baywatch,* though she told both the press and the producers that she was now willing to change her entire lifestyle if it would help her marriage or her chances of bearing a child. She was even prepared, she claimed, to give up her fantastic figure, and already had names planned for her intended family. A boy would be Rock, as in "Rock Solid," and a girl would be Cristal, after her favorite brand of champagne.

Unfortunately, Pamela's dreams of a more ordered life began to seem unattainable. Just as he had insisted on being present on the set of *Barb Wire,* Tommy began to hang around *Baywatch,* winning few friends in the process. When the script of one particular episode called for Pamela to hold hands with her former boyfriend, David Charvet, Tommy's jealousy was manifested in a temper tantrum observed by hundreds of bewildered fans watching outside the location perimeter. There were also hundreds of witnesses to another Tommy Lee outburst, this time in Connecticut when Pamela made a publicity appearance with a handsome wrestler named Shawn Michaels. The event did indeed attract publicity—though not the kind anyone probably planned or wished—when Tommy's jealousy led him to try to punch the fighter and he had to be forcibly restrained by security guards. Anecdotes of Tommy's bad behavior were plentiful, but Pamela's love apparently knew no bounds.

Yet things were beginning to go awry for Pamela. She had made her entire living from being the most wholesome, cleanest-living of sex symbols and now, for reasons beyond

Baywatch *wins the American Red Cross Spirit award*

The Baywatch *California sun and fun look*

her control, she was beginning to find her reputation tarnished. Pamela, whose contract with *Baywatch* required a wholesome image, faced being fired. Sources at *Baywatch,* which has always been promoted as a family show, said that it was "merely a matter of time." David Hasselhof was now fed up with the scandals that plagued Pamela and he knew that, popular as she was, there were plenty more beautiful blondes out there. Despite feeling increasingly threatened, Pamela chose to explain everything away with a single phrase: "Every day is New Year's Eve with Tommy."

Soon she was working on a new role, that of a secretary named Velda in a detective thriller called *Mike Hammer.* But, once again—and much to her delight—Pamela found herself pregnant. The strain of shooting both a motion picture and *Baywatch,* as well as coping with her husband, began to show and, despite her contract, she suffered obvious and dramatic weight loss. Pamela appeared to be increasingly depressed and anxious as Tommy continued to visit her film sets. The situation came to a head one afternoon when Pamela had a particularly violent fight with her husband, after which she ran into her trailer in a flood of tears. Tommy also ran off the set and Pamela ordered the production company's security men never to let him back in. Once again there was no shortage of insiders quick to scurry away and call the tabloids, who duly reported the latest episode in full Technicolor detail. As ever, neither Pamela nor Tommy rebutted their lurid accounts.

Pamela seemed calm enough once Tommy had left and carried on filming quietly for the rest of the afternoon. Then she went home. Later that evening the emergency services received a panic telephone call from her house and heard Pamela mumbling that she was by herself and that she had collapsed with "flu-like symptoms due to taking too many aspirins." An ambulance arrived soon after and she was rushed to Westlake Medical Center, but then dramatically switched to the much bigger Santa Monica Hospital some

Pamela on the beach in Baywatch *lifeguard suit*

forty miles away. The ambulance crew had found her at home alone. Though Tommy followed her straight to the hospital and told reporters that he was "out of his mind with worry," public opinion dictated that he should take the blame for the entire incident and responsibility for the fact that his wife was now lying in a hospital bed. Pamela's publicist, Anne Israel, blasted the rumors that flew all over Hollywood and said that Pamela was suffering from "exhaustion" due to her hectic work schedule. The hospital was crawling with concerned *Baywatch* public relations people, who were anxious that the reputation of the family show should not be tarnished any further. Pamela, meanwhile, tried to reassess her new self, since she was reported to have lost an alarming fifteen pounds.

But Pamela was out of the hospital soon enough, determined to make a better go of things and to renegotiate her marriage and her career. Despite this apparent resilience, however, problems continued to beset her. In October 1995 she was faced with a $5 million law suit for breach of contract. A production company called the Private Movie Company claimed that she had agreed to star in a film called *Hello, She Lied* and that she had suddenly dropped out when she was offered more money for the part in *Barb Wire.* Pamela denied this and she later won the case when the judge ruled that she had not entered into a binding contract to make the film.

By Christmas 1995, however, her relationship with Tommy appeared to have taken a slightly brighter turn. At the invitation of the British newspaper the *Sun,* the couple heralded their truce with a little jaunt to London, where they received a rapturous welcome from excited *Baywatch* fans. Pam filled in her occupation as "mommy" on the immigration form, and hordes of teenagers watched her pose for photos in a fake fur miniskirt. "Tommy and I are looking forward to a good cup of tea and eating scones and crumpets," she told her delighted fans. While the *Sun* made the most of

Pamela at the 1995 Cannes Film Festival

her trip by featuring special pictures of Pamela, *Playboy,* too, decided to cash in on her newfound fame by rereleasing old footage of her in a "brand-new" video (it was essentially a rehash of footage almost a decade old). Entitled *Playboy: The Best of Pamela Anderson,* the video sold well over half a million copies.

The trip to England and the overwhelming support of adoring fans there seemed to have done the pair some good since things then calmed down a little. Known the world over, Pamela can have little left to aim for—except, perhaps, more challenging acting roles. Over a billion viewers in 142 countries watch Pamela Anderson jog along the beach in her red swimsuit every week, yet no one really knew whether the girl from Comox had really gotten what she wanted.

She did get one thing she wanted on June 5, 1996, when she and Tommy had a son, whom they named Brandon. A few months later, however, the marriage was in trouble, and in November Pamela filed for divorce, citing irreconcilable differences and requesting joint custody of their son. Yet by the following month the couple had apparently worked out their differences, and they held a ceremony on Christmas Eve to renew their vows. Pamela declared, "This time it's forever!"

In mid-1997 she was reportedly working on a proposed syndicated series called *Fashion Force,* which she hopes will utilize her most "underexploited asset," her sense of humor. "Everybody says I'm plastic from head to toe," she has commented. "I can't stand next to a radiator or I'll melt!" Pamela, at least, seems to realize the fragility of her sex goddess status, and is able to do so with good humor. For now Pamela Anderson Lee seems happy to continue along the path her life has taken. "I'm really happy with my life," she says. "Everything is changing for the better."

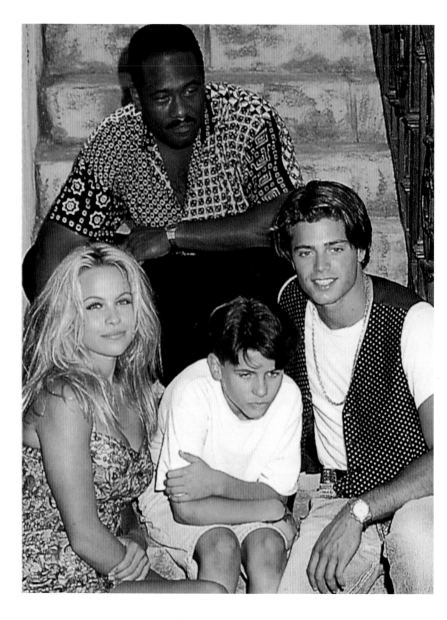

Pamela with Baywatch *cast members*

FILMOGRAPHY

1992   *Home Improvement* (television series)
1992   *Baywatch* (television series)
1993   *Snapdragon*
1995   *Hidden Paradise* (Baywatch television movie)
1995   *Barb Wire*

INDEX

INDEX